THE KING OF BANGOR

A ONE ACT PLAY

BY LEE GAMBIN

Overlook Connection Press
— 2011 —

KING OF BANGOR
A ONE ACT PLAY

Text © 2011 by Gambin's Gore Galore / Lee Gambin

Cover art © 2011 by Michael Broom

This edition is Published and © 2011 by
Overlook Connection Press
PO Box 1934, Hiram, Georgia 30141
www.overlookconnection.com
overlookcn@aol.com

First Trade Paperback Edition
ISBN-13: 978-1-892950-54-3

Book Design & Typesetting:
David G. Barnett/Fat Cat Graphic Design
www.fatcatgraphicdesign.com

A WRITER'S GRATITUDE...

A lot of people made this play possible—both in its creation on paper and then in its first run here in Melbourne, Australia... First and foremost I dedicate this play to Stephen King who first got me hooked with his New England working class vampires in *Salem's Lot*. To my mother Grace who was always there for support. To my lovely friends involved in the first readings: Alice MacNamara, Matthew Hickey, Louise Galofaro, Hande Noyan and Lisa Rae Bartolomei, and to those who got it off the ground, Georgina Tullett, Anthony Biancofiore and Dione Jospeh. And special thanks to the gang at MKA Theatre who requested this play initially. To Chris Alexander and everyone else at *Fangoria* for such awesome support. And to Molly the wonder dog, who sat waiting for me to finish writing so she could go for walkies.

Thank you
x x x

Cast of Characters:

STEPHEN KING: Male, white, middle aged, tall and with a grandiose presence, with burning intelligence.

QUEENIE: Female, white, middle aged, homely, portly build, nurturing but can be overpowering.

MR KNIGHT: Male, white, middle aged, stocky build, possibly balding, worn out.

PRINCESS: Female, white, young, small town beauty, lithe, vulnerable but with worldly intelligence.

PRINCETON: Male, white, young, lean muscular build, simple and unassuming, actively interested.

"THE KING OF BANGOR"

A one act play written by Lee Gambin

In oppressive darkness we hear the sound of a typewriter's keys being punched. At first it is slow; the keys painfully pounded out in aggressive spurts then for a moment the rhythms become more constant and consistent. There is a flow. But it is short lived. Stunted in an instant as the lights come up

We are introduced to STEPHEN KING; the famous prolific horror novelist. Dressed in a loose shirt with sleeves rolled up; the top few buttons undone and a pair of well worn jeans and sneakers; he sits at the typewriter scrutinizing it with both great admiration and utter resentment. By his side are bottles of booze; whiskey, beer, wine, gin. He also has a round mirror lying upon the table which is home to a few lines of cocaine. Bottles of pills are scattered around; some are open, ready for devouring while others look as though they have been set up in eager anticipation for a special occasion

KING: (reading from his work) The writer sat at his desk; his typewriter like a demanding metallic god longing to be worshipped. He looked over its broad little body and gently danced his fingertips across the keys.

Lights expose dark looming figures that stand behind King. The first shadowy figure is revealed: She is a middle aged woman with a rosy regal presence. She is a moderately attractive brunette, broad and sensible looking. She wears a white blouse with a lacey fringed collar, a snug black knee length skirt and a pair of black shoes with a slight heel and buckle. We will call her QUEENIE

KING: (reading) He noticed pieces of paper scattered by the deity and something caught his eye. A doodle. A foreign doodle. There was no way he sketched that.

The next figure is a young man in his early twenties. He is very tall, lightly muscled with strong facial features. He is statuesque and handsome; attentive like a soldier. He wears dark blue Levi's, slightly soiled sneakers and a clean small white t shirt. This is PRINCETON

KING: (still reading) That doodle didn't *belong* to him. (in his protagonist's voice) Ah belong! What the hell does that mean anymore? (as storyteller) The word 'belong' seemed to amuse the jaded writer.

A painfully sexual young girl appears. She is the closest to King. She is dripping with raw sensuality and seems to be completely unaware of that fact. She has strawberry blonde hair that elegantly frames her angelic features. Her arms are long and lithe like a dancer's and her legs seem to go on forever. She was once an innocent but now completely a creature in servitude of the flesh. She wears a summer dress with a light floral print. It hugs at her body; there is something slightly juvenile about her appeal, as though any man who lusted after her could be accused of pederasty. We can call her PRINCESS

KING: (reading) When a writer hands over his work to someone its suddenly owned by that person and then passed on readily available to be re-read by someone else. The work of a writer is like nobody's whore. (frustrated) Nobody's whore? What the fuck is that all about for Chrissake?

He tears the sheet of paper from his typewriter and bashes it into a ball. He tosses it to the final figure who comes into light:

The final figure is at polar opposite of King. He catches the ball of paper and unfolds it, straightening it out. This figure is a distinguished older man; at least reaching the end of his forties. He is solidly built with a thick mass of black hair. His face is tortured, a map of creases and indentations bought on from years of struggle. He wears a light blue shirt that is in desperate need of ironing, rolled up to the elbows and his light brown corduroy pants are sagging and not a good fit. His comfortable shoes

*ready to be devoured by moths. This sad, damaged oaf is known as MR.
KNIGHT.*

MR. KNIGHT: (unwrapping the ball of paper and examining
it) How about a slightly successful writer who comes back to
his hometown to work on a new book? You know, someone
who's had two or three published doosies and one best seller
and now he's on the road to writing a real personal novel…
something that takes him back to his childhood…

The others begin to offer suggestions to the struggling writer:

PRINCESS: How about a tortured teenager who is constantly
picked on by her peers…

PRINCETON: What about a creep who buys something that
takes over his life.

QUEENIE: You know a woman who commits adultery is left
out in the storm; that's one of the rules in literature. You should
use it.

PRINCETON: …And then it's a case of who owns who…

MR KNIGHT: What would happen if Dracula visited a small
coastal town in the modern age?

PRINCESS: And the girl they pick on is some kind of genius.
Or she's got some kind of hidden talent.

MR. KNIGHT: I've always liked "Peyton Place" by Grace Met-
alious. What a great book…

QUEENIE: The storm can be anything you want it to be. It
could be terrorists, a virus, a swarm of bees…

MR KNIGHT: A ghost story. How's bout a good old fashioned ghost story?

PRINCETON: An assassin who's hired to kill a little kid. Maybe like a little girl who can destroy cities. I ain't too sure on how she can destroy whole cities just yet but she can.

PRINCESS: You could write about the imaginary fears and anxieties of a troubled young family going out the window when they're faced with a quote unquote real threat...

QUEENIE: And the monster is actually just a lonely middle aged woman with delusions and obsessive needs which turn ugly.

MR. KNIGHT: A love story. Even better, a love triangle. The third party isn't exactly human.

PRINCESS: An Indian burial ground.

PRINCETON: A rabid dog.

PRINCESS: A religious zealot.

MR. KNIGHT: (slightly warning) All work and no play...

QUEENIE: An Angel of Mercy nurse who has run out of patients...so she has to improvise...

MR. KNIGHT: How about a writer who has run out of ideas?

KING: I need a drink.

MR. KNIGHT: Like I said: All work and no play...

King pours himself a drink as Queenie comes to "life."

The scene shifts and we are now in a tangible reality of some kind; Queenie has become some kind of secretary to King:

QUEENIE: How was the interview Stephen?

STEPHEN: Not as daunting as I expected. My answers seemed to ooze out.

QUEENIE: See? I told you it wouldn't be so bad.

Queenie walks over to a filing cabinet (a phone sits on the top) and goes through a mammoth amount of paper work. She fishes something out:

STEPHEN: It still wasn't the easiest thing to get through though, I'd rather try rehab again to be totally honest.

QUEENIE: (re: his drinking) Well keep this up and you might be on your way.

KING: Don't hound me, just let me be; I'm way on top of it.

QUEENIE: As you've always said.

KING: If you had a drink *with* me you wouldn't think it was such a bad pass time.

QUEENIE: Oh so now drinking has become a hobby of sorts?

KING: Absolutely. Now join me. At least have a glass of wine for Chrissake. You'll probably surprise yourself and have a good time. Come on, have a good time would ya? What are you afraid of?

QUEENIE: Shouldn't you of all people know how to answer that question? You make a living out of giving folk a good scare.

KING: Well I'm pretty stuck at the moment.

QUEENIE: You'll plough through the thickets. You always do.

KING: Did you read the interview?

QUEENIE: No.

KING: Anyone you know read the interview?

QUEENIE: No. Not that I know of. Not that I know anyone. I don't talk to people anymore Stephen, you know that. I've made it a conscious decision to be the misanthrope that I am. It's easier.

KING: Fair enough.

QUEENIE: Did you speak to Tabitha?

KING: She's good. She's good. Her and the kids are in Portland at the moment seeing some relative I've never heard of. But I know she's over there as an excuse to give me room to write. She's a good woman that Tabby.

QUEENIE: If we could all have partners that were *that* understanding.

KING: She's the best. She hasn't called just yet, but she's the best.

QUEENIE: She'll call when she gets there. It's a bit of a drive.

KING: (pouring another drink) Gotta stock up on more booze soon...

QUEENIE: She's worried about you.

KING: Worried? She shouldn't be worried. I'm fine.

QUEENIE: You're drinking too much Steve. It's not good.

KING: Come on. I always drink when I work.

QUEENIE: And in between work and just before sleep and in the early hours of the morning. And I'm sure if I navigated your dreamscape you'd be sinking into your gin and vodka just as happily.

KING: The last thing I'd need is you in my dreams.

QUEENIE: Jeez you're lucky I'm not sensitive or I'd take that as a severe insult.

KING: Ahh there I go again, not choosing the right words...I need to learn to shut my big ugly trap...always with the wrong words...

QUEENIE: Stick to putting them to paper. That's where you shine.

KING: It's the drugs. Not so much the drinking. Tabby's concerned with the drugs.

QUEENIE: No shit.

KING: But just like the booze, I'm way on top of it all.

QUEENIE: Really just?

KING: Really just.

QUEENIE: She has every right to be worried but I'm not prepared to sound like a broken record player, I'm here to work for you and remind you about this.

She hands him the document she fished out

KING: What the hell is this?

QUEENIE: A contract.

KING: Contract?

QUEENIE: From Warner Bros.

KING: Warner hey?

QUEENIE: Yet another movie deal. A walk in the park really.

KING: Ooh…let's see how the big ole studios wanna massacre my work hey?

QUEENIE: They've done pretty well in the past. Be nice. Play nice.

Princeton comes DS and rests by the filing cabinet. He wedges his hands into his jeans pockets and looks slightly concerned. It doesn't suit him, but nonetheless he is concerned:

PRINCETON: I'm worried about my best friend Arnie.

King and Queenie continue:

KING: (scanning the contract put before him) I like this producer, I like this screenwriter, I like this approach.

QUEENIE: So I take it you approve?

KING: Do I have a choice?

QUEENIE: You know you do. Now is there anything I need to start on? Mail? More press junk?

Queenie puts on her spectacles and sits by King's side sorting through mail while King grabs hold of a twenty dollar note from his chewed up wallet and begins to roll it up

KING: You could help me get this novel on the way.

PRINCETON: He and I have known each other since we were kids and we were a team ya know? Inseparable.

MR.KNIGHT: (from a far, to King) Married to your work pal. Stay obsessed.

Princess emerges from US and ends at polar opposite to Princeton. The two attractive youngsters frame the writer and his long suffering assistant Princess and Princeton begin to share dialogue, discussing troubled people they know; living and recently deceased:

PRINCESS: (obnoxiously) Well I knew Carrie White for a long time and she deserved to die. (angry statement, giving the bird) Eat shit in hell Carrie White.

King stretches his arms over his typewriter

KING: Any ideas?

QUEENIE: It's your baby Stephen. They're all your babies.

KING: What kind of team are we?

QUEENIE: We're not a team. You're on your own.

KING: Well ain't that a shame? Now lets help out the insomnia shall we?

He snorts a long line

QUEENIE: You know with the amount of money you spend on that shit you could get yourself a new typewriter. Or better yet a laptop or something from *this* century.

MR. KNIGHT: All work and no play makes Jack a dull boy.

KING: And give up ole Bessie? Never! I can't part with her.

PRINCESS: (as if being interviewed by police) Carrie was a scapegoat sure. She was a joke to every one. The entire school hated her.

PRINCETON: As we got older things got a lot harder for Arnie. The poor guy was beaten up and teased by fucks like Buddy Repperton and his jerk off friends but I was always there to stand up for him.

PRINCESS: (to Princeton) Why would you bother being friends with someone like Arnie Cunningham?

PRINCETON: (offended) Huh?

PRINCESS: You're high school royalty for fuck's sake; football hero and campus stud and you still let ugly weedy Arnie hang by your side? That's just plain weird.

PRINCETON: What the fuck are you on about, Arnie's my best friend.

PRINCESS: Yeah well its odd. Such an unlikely pairing really. Dennis Guilder the all American guy and Arnie Cunningham the born loser. Didn't the others call him Cuntingham? Wasn't that it?

King pours himself another drink and starts typing

KING: (as he types, reading what he pounds out) The other girls laughed and threw feminine hygiene products at her, foreign objects to the likes of Margaret White's sad little sap who was bunched up in a ball in the corner of the shower…(rethinking) no, wait on (typing, reading) the others laughed and called her names, screaming at her like crazed harpies…

Princess and Princeton now notice King. Queenie continues to work on mountains of paper work

PRINCESS: She deserved it mister. She was such a retard.

KING: (studying his work) Nasty kids, nasty games…

PRINCESS: Are you listening to me? Do you know what that bitch did to the whole town? How many fucking people died?

King turns to Princess and stares right at her. He takes his glasses off and angrily points to her. He wants to spew out hateful words but he puts his glasses back on and goes back to typing

KING: I've known horrible kids like you all my goddamn life miss. What Carrie did was understandable.

PRINCESS: How can you say that?

KING: You're lucky to be one of the survivors. I could of killed you off. You could have been yet another casualty of the Black Prom as I so profoundly coined it.

PRINCESS: (slight taunting) What are you working on now Stevey? More sad unfortunates who get their revenge on their tormentors? It's such a bankable plot device.

KING: It's more than a device sweetheart, it's what I know.

Princess's taunting slowly morphs into flirtation:

PRINCESS: Was it really that intense for you? High school? Was it such an ordeal?

KING: Yes. In many ways I was Carrie.

PRINCESS: Oh come on, I don't buy that.

KING: I only wish I had *her* power. (motioning to his type-writer) This ain't too good a substitute.

PRINCESS: It's monstrous and horrible and unforgivable, what she did.

KING: They all deserved it.

PRINCETON: Mr. King, Arnie doesn't deserve the same fate.

KING: Arnie has the power too Dennis and her name is Christine.

PRINCESS: Christine? Who's Christine?

Princeton Xes over to Princess:

PRINCETON: Arnie and I were driving home one day from school ya see and he spotted this piece of junk in a lot near by and he, well, he fell in love.

PRINCESS: Oh good Jesus who would love Arnie Cunting-ham?

KING: Christine. That's who.

PRINCETON: Did you know that Arnie has one amazing talent Norma? Something only a few people know. Something that really pisses his parents off because they want him to focus on his studies so he can get into law or medicine or something important—

PRINCESS: Managing to repulse everyone that comes into contact with him is hardly a talent Dennis.

KING: Cars. Arnie can do wonders with cars. Fix 'em up, dress 'em up then rev 'em up...

PRINCETON: He's a master mechanic. And Christine was the perfect project. It was love at first sight.

KING: (typing, reading) This story is a love triangle. It is about Arnie Cunningham, Leigh Cabbott and Christine a 1958 red Plymouth Fury.

PRINCETON: Arnie is my best friend and I wanna look out for him that's all.

KING: Let him do what he wants Guilder. Back off.

PRINCETON: But don't you see? It's damaging. He's obsessed with this thing and its fucked. It's not good for him, it really fuckin' isn't.

KING: How do you know what's good or not good for him Guilder? You've had it easy you're whole life; you've had yourself an easy fucking run pal.

PRINCETON: You don't know me well enough to say that.

KING: What are you talking about? You're my meaningless creation. And I know the kind of kid you are Dennis all too very well. And depressingly I know the kind of sorry ass kid Arnie is as well. He's suffered from day one. And you know that. If you say you're his best friend than you *should* know that. You've got your athleticism and charms, smarts and good looks and everyone can tell that you're a good kid just from lookin' at you but as soon as they see pimple faced ugly Arnie Cuntingham they see a born loser. A sucker. Someone who really needs to be put out of his misery sooner than later. Someone destined for failure.

PRINCETON: He's not a loser.

KING: Come on Dennis, *even* as his best friend, deep down you see nothing great in the horizon for him. But now he has this car and that makes him feel less of a loser. So let him keep it. Don't get in between him and Christine.

PRINCETON: Well I don't think I can. I want to, but I can't.

KING: You can't interfere with what goes on between 'em Dennis. Let him go. He belongs to her now. To that red '58 Plymouth Fury.
PRINCETON: You're not so much a great help Mr. King.

KING: I never promised to be.

PRINCESS: (once again as if talking to a police man) I remember the day after the shower incident and I was in study hall with Christine Hargensen and Helen Shyres and some of the other girls, I can't clearly remember who was there, but, I do remember Carrie coming down the hall. Her hair parted in the middle wet with grease and her shoulders slumped...

PRINCETON:
Arnie's no longer
the Arnie I know. He's starting
to wear these threads that just
aren't him; its as if in Christine's
transformation from junk heap
to a classic beauty of an
automobile, Arnie too has changed.

PRINCESS:
...her arms tightly
gripping her
second hand books
that I just know
she had to hide
from her nut job
of a mother...

KING: (to Queenie) Hey you remember that girl that I told you about from my old high school, the one that kind of inspired the look and demeanor and what not for Carrie...?

QUEENIE: (not even looking up from paper work) Mmm?

KING: Real back water thing. More dirt poor than me.

QUEENIE: Yes I remember. She had that mother that was obsessed with buying lottery tickets.

KING: (impressed with Queenie) Ha! Like an elephant. (he kisses her head) Lottery obsessions quickly became religious fanaticism.

PRINCESS: (continuing) So anyway, we all stared at her, hating her, because the stupid bitch got us all detention for a week for the incident in the shower room and Chris Hargensen had been suspended and not allowed to attend— (choking) attend the senior prom.

KING: Well she shot herself.

QUEENIE: (now all ears) Who did?

KING: That girl. The weirdo no body liked. She grew up to be even more miserable. I heard it from one of the dads down at the Little Leagues that she shot herself in the guts. Poor little fool.

PRINCESS: (continuing) When Carrie walked past us, Chris told her to eat shit and the window behind us shattered. In one mighty blow it just cracked and shattered. I think Helen cut her arm from it. She was leaning on the ledge. Carrie darted off down the hall like the nervous little shit she was.

PRINCETON: Buddy Repperton's body was found completely massacred. His arms were broken, his legs were brutally sliced up, his face was an unrecognizable mess. It was the result of a hit and run. But I ain't too sure if the car did a runner straight away. Not with *that* damage done. The police report said it was a malicious attack. As if the car repeatedly rammed itself into Buddy...

PRINCESS: (in a painful daze) I saw Frieda Jason's neck twist and snap when she went flying into the gymnasium's wall—

PRINCETON: Buddy Repperton was Arnie's number one enemy. He was mean to him from day one.

PRINCESS: I saw Rhonda Wilson and George Dawson fry in a shot of electricity; their skin burning and cooking, blistering and turning black...

PRINCETON: Every thing changed when he bought Christine.

Princess stands behind King

PRINCESS: Stephen, you gave her those powers and it cost every one their lives...

PRINCETON: Christine can't be destroyed. She's doing everything she can for Arnie. I fear the worst for Leigh Cabbott.

KING: (I know the truth of the matter) You wanna fuck Leigh Cabbott.

PRINCETON: (defensive) Leigh Cabbott is Arnie's girl.

KING: (truth) *Christine* is Arnie's girl.

PRINCESS: Your writing is like Carrie White's telekinesis Stephen. It's your gift.

PRINCETON: But it can destroy a whole town.

Queenie grabs a near by pad and reads the notes:

QUEENIE: "Firestarter"?

KING: Uhh yeah, umm, it's about a little pigtailed girl called Charlie McGee, who can't really control her 'talent'.

QUEENIE: Pyrokinesis?

King smiles at her, as if she got the joke:

QUEENIE: Just a stab in the dark.

KING: She's the result of a secret government agency's drug testing. I haven't fleshed it out yet; but I'm on my way... just give me time...

QUEENIE: You have all the time in the world.

PRINCESS: Your writing is like Christine. It cancels out the fodder that gets in your way and builds you and shapes you.

PRINCETON: But it can shape you into something sinister. I'm scared of Arnie now Mr. King. I'm real scared. I've never actually been scared in my whole life; not really, no football match, no date with some chick, nothing to do with drinking or driving or my parents or my friends or school or my grades, nothing has ever made me nervous or scared. I mean properly scared. But right now…it's all—different.

And I'm not only terrified for Arnie's sake, but for everyone else's. Every one who loves him. They seem to be…

PRINCESS: Fodder to cancel out.

PRINCETON: (clarity) Yeah.

Princeton and Princess disappear into darkness as Mr. Knight comes to 'life'. He moves toward King carrying a six pack:

MR KNIGHT: Hey sorry I'm late.

KING: You made it! Jesus Christ I was gonna send out a search party.

QUEENIE: And you're lookin' at her right here.

KING: (to Mr Knight re: Queenie) She makes for a good looking bloodhound don't she buddy?

The sound of a baseball game on television is heard and a shaft of light from an o.s television set hits Mr. Knight

MR KNIGHT: Did I miss anything?

KING: To be honest I've been working like a dog, slaving away here to even notice.

MR KNIGHT: That ain't like you Steve. The Red Sox are a big part of your life for Chrissake.

KING: Ahh yeah, they were.

MR KNIGHT: What you working on?

KING: A novel.

MR KNIGHT: (no shit) Yes…? And it's about…?

QUEENIE: He hasn't decided.

MR KNIGHT: Ahh. One of those periods huh?

QUEENIE: Care to dig him out of it?

KING: Care for something to go with those beers buddy?

King tosses him a bottle of speed pills. Mr Knight catches them they same way he caught the piece of paper earlier

MR KNIGHT: (reading label) Dexedrine.

KING: Damn straight. You'll enjoy the game and those beers a thousand times more.

MR KNIGHT: Amphetamines so early in the day Stephen?

KING: (to Queenie) He always calls me Stephen when he's disappointed in me.

MR KNIGHT: Folk'd think you were a truck driver or something the way you down these fuckers.

KING: I am. Cruising down the highway waiting for that interesting hitchhiker to pick up who'll inspire some words for me to string together. Some scary words. And if the words don't scare 'em then they better repulse 'em. Make 'em sick. Ohh yes my man I *am* one helluva truck driver.

MR KNIGHT: Well I'll stick to beer if its all the same thanks.

Mr Knight places the pills back on the table. Queenie stands up and moves to USR, dimly lit. King continues to type and drink. He unscrews the pill box and takes three. Downing them with scotch

MR. KNIGHT: Its your youngest's birthday sometime soon ain't it?

KING: Sure is.

MR KNIGHT: How old?

KING: Eight.

MR KNIGHT: Jeez Louise its already been that long huh?

KING: Yep.

MR KNIGHT: Doing anything for him?

KING: Tabitha's givin' him a party. Right here at home.

MR KNIGHT: Well I'll be sure to bring my kids down.

KING: You better.

MR KNIGHT: God, the eldest got under my skin just two months ago.

KING: Oh yeah?

MR KNIGHT: The damn whippersnapper got into my paper work for the stock take this month. Decided to make little ole paper dolls outta 'em.

King starts to laugh, still busily typing

KING: Ha! What a hoot!

MR KNIGHT: It's my wife's fault. She taught him how to make the darn things and when she ran out of paper the little tike got up to my den and had his way with a month's worth of work. Shredded to pieces they are now.

KING: Ahh ya gotta love kids.

MR KNIGHT: Of course. Of course I love my kids. But that kind of thing can make you just get real...well...

KING: (suddenly interested) What?

MR KNIGHT: Well I hate working on that crap Steve. You know that.

KING: Numbers. Urgh. They scare the hell outta me.

MR KNIGHT: Exactly. Well, when I finally get through the fuckin' shit I can rest as ease...

KING: Sink a few beers...

MR KNIGHT: And just relax. But that little—

KING: Go on.

MR KNIGHT: Well what if one of yours came in and you were half way through, or even worse, three quarters of the way through a novel and one of your own thought he'd grab a couple of Crayolas and draw all over them there sheets of paper. What would you do?

KING: Well I'd—

MR KNIGHT: And don't think rationally about it, just go instinctively, as if your kid was some grown man, a complete stranger fucking with your work. What would you do?

KING: I'd bash the living hell outta him.

MR KNIGHT: Exactly.

KING: But every one gets frustrated with their kids pal, you don't suddenly become saintly as soon as you become a parent. There are times I wanna throttle the throats of those little bastards but I love 'em...

MR KNIGHT: But there's that thought. And that thought is there. It's always there.

Mr Knight slowly morphs into Jack Torrance from King's novel "The Shining". King becomes nervous, frightened:

KING: What are you saying? What are you suggesting?

MR KNIGHT: Wendy and I never talk about it, but I can tell that it bothers her still to this day.

KING: Oh yeah...? What?

MR KNIGHT: After my boy did that, after he shredded those papers to smithereens I lashed out. I lashed out big time too.

KING: You—ya hit him?

MR KNIGHT: Gave him one big wallop across the throat. He bruised up pretty much straight away.

KING: Oh man, that's real bad...

MR KNIGHT: Wendy got to him and asked if I did that and of course he told her...

KING: Real real bad...

MR KNIGHT: She baby's that kid. She always has.

KING: I'd never hit my kid, never ever...

MR KNIGHT: Oh but you might. Who knows Stevey boy, you may even wanna kill the fuckers and even chop pretty little wifey up into pieces too...

KING: Fuck off...get the fuck outta here...

MR KNIGHT: All work and no play Stephen.

KING: Stop it. Get lost.

MR KNIGHT: Have another drink.

KING: I will. I fucking well will!

MR KNIGHT: Imagine what those little monsters can do to you Stevey; tearing you to shreds, ripping you apart!

KING: Get lost! Just fuck right off will ya?

Princeton races in exhausted. He is sweating. He has changed from Dennis Guilder to someone from the 'real' world. He carries with him a parcel wrapped up in a brown paper bag. It's the shape of a book

PRINCETON: Stephen I got here as soon as I could.

KING: Jesus Christ you scared the shit outta me.

King's fear is swallowed and he is relieved its Princeton

PRINCETON: First edition. "The Dead Zone". All yours.

KING: Ahh nothing finer then a fresh off the print first ed.

MR Knight leaves his beers for King and joins Queenie

PRINCETON: I been running.

KING: I can tell. (staring at him) And I can smell.

PRINCETON: I thought you needed it by a certain time and I waited for ages at the book store, and the lady there wasn't helpful—

KING: Wasn't she?

PRINCETON: And the fans. My God have you met them?

KING: Certainly not.

PRINCETON: I don't know how you do book signings but their rabid. Like rabid dogs.

KING: Hmmm….rabies….

King jots down a note on a near by piece of paper

PRINCETON: Can I get a drink of water please?

KING: Water?

PRINCETON: Yeah.

KING: What's that?

Princeton looks slightly confused, he has finally gotten his breath back though

KING: My poor attempt at a bad joke, all apologies; but you sure you don't wanna beer instead?

PRINCETON: Oh I'd love one.

KING: Help yourself.

Princeton takes a beer. King puts a fresh piece of paper into the typewriter, rolling it down

KING: Did you know when an animal gets rabies they cant stomach water. In fact rabies is often sometimes called hydrophobia. As in the fear of hydration. Or the fear of water.

PRINCETON: Oh I ain't scared of water, no way. I'm a big fan. It's essential for guys like me.

KING: Uh huh.

PRINCETON: But I do prefer beer. Especially on hot days like this. But I really shouldn't drink while I'm training.

KING: You in training?

PRINCETON: Yeah Mr. King. I'm a long distance runner. Have been for a little while now.

KING: (back to work) How interesting.

PRINCETON: I've told you before.

KING: Oh yeah?

PRINCETON: Yeah. You must of forgotten. But why would you remember that, I mean you're so busy and everything.

KING: What else you do? Besides run and run errands for yours truly?

PRINCETON: Well nothing much…

KING: Nothing much?

PRINCETON: I mean its Bangor. What is there to do?

KING: Don't underestimate small towns kid.

PRINCETON: I was born here and I've lived here all my life so what I do is what I've done from day one. That's it. That's all. Nothing else.

KING: Besides running.

PRINCETON: Yep.

KING: (writing down another idea) The running man…

PRINCETON: May I have another beer?

KING: You downed that one already kid?

PRINCETON: I drink real fast.

KING: Well you might have to be an occasional drinking buddy of mine down the track.

King offers another beer:

PRINCETON: Thanks.

KING: You ever wanted to run away to another town kid?

PRINCETON: Oh yeah. All the time. And not just some other shitty place here in Maine but like to Boston or New York or something.

KING: Would be nice huh?

PRINCETON: Well you tell me. You've been all those places. Are they? I mean are they nice?

KING: Yeah, give or take. But I'll always come home. Bangor is where the heart is.

PRINCETON: Yeah. I understand. I mean, Bangor *is* home and as much as I complain about there bein' nuttin' to do 'round here I really couldn't leave it for good.

KING: Married to home turf.

Princess takes the package and unwraps it slowly. Her demeanor is pleasant, sweet, serene. She takes the book into her hands and it is not a copy of "The Dead Zone" but an untitled book with a picture of Princeton on the inlay.

She sits on the ground and reads. The prettiest of pictures

Princeton watches her and his demeanor changes. He becomes far more self-confident and not at all jittery as he previously was. He walks over to her, King watches them:

Princess notices Princeton watching and smiles but then realizes that he is the writer of the book she's reading:

PRINCESS: Hey, you're him aren't you? On the sleeve of my book? The writer? That's you isn't it?

PRINCETON: Well that depends. Are you enjoying it?

KING: She'll lie to you.

PRINCESS: Yeah. I am.

KING: She's lying.

PRINCESS: It's real good.

PRINCETON: Then I am the writer and that picture is a picture of me. Although why I chose to wear that shirt is beyond me…oh and I look so serious.

PRINCESS: You're a native aren't you? You were born here, right?

PRINCETON: Yes mam. Says so on the inlay.

He sits down with her

PRINCESS: What you doing back?

PRINCETON: I've come home to work.

KING: Can't cut ties kiddo. Married to home turf.

PRINCETON: You a local girl?

PRINCESS: Born and bred. Can't you tell? Don't I have that small town coastal Maine vibe? It's a distinct look you know?

PRINCETON: I've forgotten what it was like. But it's all coming back to me now.

KING: Enjoy it while you can buddy.

PRINCESS: I've moved once or twice. The first time was to New York and then a year later to Boston, but for some reason I've always ended up here again.

PRINCETON: What brings you back?

PRINCESS: Not sure.

KING: Home is where the heart is. Don't underestimate small towns.

PRINCESS: I'm a teacher. Just at the local high school. I teach art.

PRINCETON: Good stuff. I'm glad someone with artistic appreciation is enjoying that drivel I churned out those many years ago. You know, I was about to can that book. Tossed it right into the garbage I did.

KING: But it was saved. Rescued.

PRINCESS: But it's so good. And critically acclaimed, and popular; its a best seller for goodness sake.

PRINCETON: Eh. It don't do much for me.

KING: So hard on yourself. So down on yourself.

PRINCETON: So what you do for fun in this ghost town?

KING: It ain't a ghost town yet buddy. And it'll be worse than that soon enough.

PRINCESS: Not much. There isn't much to do. It says here you're married. Your wife in town with you?

PRINCETON: She's passed away since then.

PRINCESS: Oh. I'm sorry.

PRINCETON: What about you? Boyfriend? I assume there's no hubby with the lack of gold or silver wrapped 'round that finger of yours.

PRINCESS: It'd be pewter in this town.

KING: Cheap kids, cheap thrills.

PRINCETON: No one for the local art teacher?

PRINCESS: There's one guy that hangs around. But he's ancient history now.

PRINCETON: Really?

KING: Small towns have their secrets.

PRINCESS: Oh he gets lonely now and then and I—well I help him out…

PRINCETON: A living breathing cure to the small town blues huh?

PRINCESS: Hardly. Everything is done out of boredom here.

PRINCETON: And that's ninety nine percent of the reason why I became a writer Miss-?

PRINCESS: Norton. Susan Norton.

PRINCETON: Oh Doctor Norton's girl?

KING: Old friends. Old ties.

PRINCETON: I wonder if he'll remember me.

PRINCESS: Daddy never forgets a face.

KING: Tell her about the house kid. The house from your childhood. The main reason you're back in town.

PRINCETON: Do you know the Marsten house?

PRINCESS: Who doesn't?

PRINCETON: That notorious huh?

PRINCESS: Definitely. Every town needs a haunted house. It keeps the local kids occupied. It's either that or cheap boxed wine and pot.

KING: I need another drink.

PRINCETON: I was one of those curious kids. I was dared to go in there.

PRINCESS: It gives me the creeps.

PRINCETON: I saw unspeakable horrors in there Susan… stuff that stays with you forever.

KING: The beauty of east coast New Englanders can easily be forgotten but images of death and decay can scar you for life…

PRINCETON: Who owns the place now?

PRINCESS: Some antiques dealer.

PRINCETON: An out of Towner?

KING: Definitely. Way out of town.

PRINCESS: Judging by his suits and the shipments I'd say he's of good stock so yes, an utter stranger to these parts. His business partner is due to arrive anytime soon too. I think they'll be living together in the Marsten house. I hope they're gay, it'll add some spice to this dull ole town and give the local gossips something to whisper about. Not that they don't whisper 'bout anyone else; especially those who aren't yet married or with a decent trade under their belt—hey hang on a second, is the Marsten house the reason why you're here? Are you writing about it? You gonna tackle some kind of horror story? A contemporary American gothic chiller by Ben Mears?

PRINCETON: (he's become smitten by her) Hey can we do dinner? I'm staying at Eva Miller's boarding house. There's a kitchen there and hopefully the local drunk is out for the night—

KING: So many secrets. Small towns are prone to secrecy.

PRINCESS: Oh Weasel. He's a drunk but he's a darling. He and Eva Miller used to date. Can you believe that?

KING: And they will be married. In the after life.

PRINCESS: I can do better than dinner at Eva's boarding house. How about dinner at my place? Daddy will want to see you again and I'd love mother to meet a published writer. She thinks the arts are a waste of time.

KING: This town will soon know darkness…

PRINCESS: Then once dinner is done I can show you what the local high school art teachers do for fun. There's a couple of bars 'round the place as you'd recall, the movies in Bangor—

PRINCETON: How about the lake?

PRINCESS: Mr. Mears how direct. You know the lake…?

PRINCETON: The lake is something I remember all too very well.

PRINCESS: The lake it is then.

KING: The prodigal son returns.

PRINCESS: Well Mr. Mears—

PRICETON: Ben. Please.

PRINCESS: Well Ben I think there's nothing more to say than: welcome back to 'Salem's Lot.

They kiss

KING: Everything will stay the same forever in 'Salem's Lot. You'll see.

A telephone rings. It is piercing and annoying. It causes some dogs to bark. They bark loudly and angrily

This is the first time King gets up and moves to it. It is sitting on top of the filing cabinet

He is the only one lit

KING: (into phone) Yeah? Hang on I can't hear you. (calling out to dogs) Quiet babies daddy's on the phone! (back into phone, they start to settle) Yeah? Hey, yeah, how you doin'? Of course I'm ok, why does every one insist on asking me that for Chrissake? (a beat)Yeah sure come on over, they could do with the exercise and I ain't got time at the moment, I'm stuck in the middle of a fucking forest and the thickets are big and black that I need a proper sword to cut my way through if you catch my drift however the fuck you catch drifts; yep, I'll see ya in a bit. Bye.

He hangs up and staggers back to his god. He looks over his pills and carefully selects a bottle, prying it open and swallowing a couple. He washes it down with one of Mr Knight's beers

Princess approaches, chipper, very alive, like a ray of sunshine; its as if she doesn't stop to breath when she talks:

PRINCESS: The door was right on open so I just came through Mr. King but you ought to be careful 'bout that kind of thing I mean so many crazy people are out there that they would just walk right inside just the way I did but instead of being here to walk your dogs they'd be here to steal from you or beat you up or kill you or something along those lines…

KING: The dogs are waitin' for ya.

PRINCESS: I read somewhere that dogs can sense people approaching from long distances and the way they can tell that people are approaching is just from the scent in the air…

KING: You want a sedative?

PRINCESS: Oh no no, Mr. King I'm perfectly fine, plus its nearing exams time and I really have to be on top of my game even though its always fun to blow off steam and binge drink and the like but I can't be partied out too much these coming weeks…

KING: What do you plan to do with your future?

She's suddenly stumped:

PRINCESS: What?

KING: Your future? Got any plans?

PRINCESS: Plans?

KING: College? A job?

PRINCESS: Oh Christ, I haven't really thought about any of that...

She sits down, slumped, now depressed

KING: Well, dogs will always need to be worked.

King sits down. He starts typing

PRINCESS: Yeah. They will.

KING: I wouldn't stress sweetheart, there's plenty of time. Hey look I was starving and barely surviving for years, it wasn't until my mid thirties that I started to reap in the goods. You got shit loads of time. Enjoy it.

She grabs his fingers and stops him from typing

PRINCESS: (suddenly deathly serious) When I reach my thirties I'll become invisible. There won't be any reason for me to exist really. I'll start to miss college and miss being single and miss not being a mother. Oh what a thought. What a horrible thought. To resent your own baby, to look at the child you've given birth to with great disdain and annoyance, a living annoyance, a living reminder that everything is not the same and that you're no longer the Donna you knew but some alien deathly bored outta her wits sod known only as mamma or mommy or ma.

KING: I gotta keep working, ya mind letting my hand go?

PRINCESS: It's that white noise. Can you hear it?

KING: The what?

PRINCESS: You know when a television set is on somewhere in a room but the sound is down and you can't see it though; like you're in the kitchen and the TV is in the living room and its on but you cant hear it but you can—do you know what I'm trying to say...?

KING: White noise, yeah I know what white noise is, now let go of—

PRINCESS: (slowly adult) That's what becomes of my life Stephen. That's what fills my days and nights. White noise. Can you blame me for running into another man's arms? Can you blame me for wanting to feel attractive and useful and interesting and to be the Donna I was; because I was interesting and fun and lovely goddamnit, I wasn't just some lowly housewife stuck with a kid and being there for a husband who's preoccupied with his fucking career...Jesus Christ!

KING: Come on calm down, let me go will ya?

The dogs start barking again

PRINCESS: (building into foaming frenzy) Oh Stephen help me out please. Before it gets to that point, just help me out. Teach me to be content and happy and completely satisfied with the husband who cares for me and provides for me and the kid who I do adore, I do, I do adore, I do, I do, but if I fuck up and if I let myself do that with *him*, that fucking man that fixes something inside of me, God knows why but he does, he just makes me feel alive again but its wrong; oh and if it continues then please, please I beg of you to let that rabid dog teach me a lesson. Let that rabid dog tear into my flesh with its foaming mouth and bloodstained teeth and may the hydrophobia run rampant through my veins! Call him something memorable! Call him something that will haunt me forever, call him something that will remind me that I ruined something that was truly wonderful and warm and safe!

King breaks from her grasp and types dramatically:

KING: (singing) C-U-J-O! And Cujo was his name-o!

Princess is calm. She smiles at him

PRINCESS: Perfect.

She kisses him on the cheek

PRINCESS: Happy writing.

The others circle him

MR KNIGHT: A dead cat comes back to life...

PRINCETON: A psychic who helps the fuzz track down some psychopath...

QUEENIE: I've always loved the movies of Bert I. Gordon. He did all those big monster movies.

PRINCETON: How about a writer who's trying to do something different but he just can't because he's so well received in a particular style of...

PRINCESS: And the kid is like floating in mid air and tapping on the window...

MR KNIGHT: All work…

QUEENIE: A circle of circumstance all leads up to one event…

PRINCETON: Every body's scared of clowns for fuck's sake; I mean look at 'em!

PRINCESS: …and the kid is tapping on the window saying "Let me in, the master commands it"…

MR KNIGHT: No play…

PRINCESS: …but the weirdest thing about that is that the kid has been dead for like a week…

PRINCETON: What about werewolves?

QUEENIE: Religious sects?

MR KNIGHT: Greasers?

PRINCETON: Monsters in the closet?

QUEENIE: How about linking the stories? Two characters from two separate novels mention the same hotel they once stayed at…

MR. KNIGHT: Necrophilia? Rape? Incest? Pedophilia? Scatology?

PRINCETON: Bad dreams?

PRINCESS: Bad parenting?

QUEENIE: Bad acid trip?

MR. KNIGHT: Bad writing?

PRINCETON: Helping out a friend the best way you can…

PRINCESS: Being punished for the mistakes you've made…

PRINCETON: Coming home to write a novel…

PRINCESS: Channeling your secret gift…

MR KNIGHT: Jack's a dull boy.

Queenie breaks out of the moment and resumes her old persona; that of the assistant. She looks concerned with King and approaches him:

QUEENIE: Steve? Steve you ok? (beat) Have you heard from Tabitha and the kids?

KING: Nope. Not yet. I'm sure they're doin' fine.

QUEENIE: You need anything?

KING: Yeah.

QUEENIE: What is it? What can I get you?

KING: I need a drink.

He pours himself another drink

QUEENIE: Look after yourself. I'm off for the rest of the day.

KING: Toodles.

Queenie is enveloped by darkness

Mr. Knight stands over King's shoulder as he drinks and slowly types

MR KNIGHT: Hi.

KING: Who are you?

MR KNIGHT: The door was left open so I just thought—

KING: You thought wrong buddy get lost.

MR KNIGHT: Well I really wanted to talk to you Mr. King.

KING: I ain't interested. I'm working here.

MR KNIGHT: Well that's the reason I turned up. That's what I want to talk to you about. Your work.

KING: I'm gonna call the police.

King goes to the phone. Mr Knight stops him with:

MR KNIGHT: The work of a writer is like nobody's whore.

KING: What?

MR KNIGHT: That's just something I wrote. I'm somewhat of a bedroom novelist.

KING: You're lying.

MR KNIGHT: No I ain't lying. I'm deadly serious.

KING: Who are you?

MR KNIGHT: (sadly amused) Who am I? That's not important. Sadly, it's not important at all. But it could have been. I could have been the well known much loved writer everyone raves about. But I'm not. I'll always be the bedroom novelist. Stuck in his house writing stuff that'll never be read by the likes of anyone.

KING: Look I'll give you three seconds to get outta here—

MR KNIGHT: (dead seriousness) I wrote "Carrie".

KING: You what?

MR KNIGHT: I was the guy that penned that classic.

KING: What are you talking about?

MR KNIGHT: I wrote the first draft of "Carrie" and you found it and you ripped it off.

KING: You're crazy.

Mr Knight turns menacing

MR KNIGHT: Oh I can be. You want me to go crazy? I can get as fucking crazy as Jack…you know? From "The Shining"?

KING: Let me guess, you wrote that too?

MR KNIGHT: Damn fucking straight!

KING: Get lost.

MR KNIGHT: I wrote these stories and you stole them off me! you made millions from 'em and I still live alone in that fucking project—

KING: (counting fast) One two three, you're out.

He picks up the phone quickly but Mr Knight as this crazed man lifts up a gun, aiming it straight at him:

MR KNIGHT: Put the phone down Mr. King.

KING: What the fuck?

MR KNIGHT: Put the phone down and pick up a pen and do the best writing you can do.

KING: What do you want from me?

MR KNIGHT: I want you to write me a cheque. A cheque for five million dollars. It ain't too much to ask for seeing as you ripped me off for everything I wrote.

KING: You're deranged.

MR KNIGHT: All work and no play made me that way. Now write!

King goes to his desk and slowly gets a cheque book and starts to write

MR KNIGHT: How you can sleep at night knowing that those stories you sold weren't really yours. My God...

KING: Who do I make it out to?

MR KNIGHT: What?

KING: Who do I write the cheque for? What's your name?

MR KNIGHT: My name?

KING: Yes, you're name!

MR KNIGHT: I—It's not important.

King's fear turns to puzzlement. Before he can react Princeton approaches; he's the errands boy from earlier. He sees the situation and wrestles Mr Knight to the ground

MR KNIGHT: Let me go! Get the fuck off me!

KING: Oh man! Thank fuck!

PRINCETON: You alright Mr. King? You ain't hurt are you?

KING: I'm fine, just keep that asshole down while I—

King goes to the phone and dials. As he dials Princeton exits with Mr Knight

King turns around they're gone

He decides to hang up

He goes to his desk and pours another drink

He contemplates the other line of cocaine and begins to roll the cheque up and hen he snorts

Enter Queenie. She is meek and slightly shy; grinning nervously: she is meeting her idol. She carries a copy of the same book that Princess was reading earlier. She also has a marker at hand

QUEENIE: Hello Mr. King. I'm you're number one fan.

KING: How'd you—?

QUEENIE: The young girl let me in.

KING: What girl?

QUEENIE: She says she walks your dogs when you're working on a novel. And I can see that you're in over your head at the moment. I'm very excited to read it. I just love your work.

KING: She shouldn't of let you in here. This is private property.

QUEENIE: And you're a very private person. I know that. I know everything about you.

King reaches for the phone

QUEENIE: Oh please, please don't be scared of lil' ole me. I'm nothing to be scared of. Ha! What a hoot! I'm just a fan who has your most recent novel here with her and a marker and I'd just love it if you—?

KING: Autograph?

QUEENIE: It would be an honor.

KING: Then you'll leave?

QUEENIE: I'm interrupting a work in progress aren't I?

KING: You already know you are.

QUEENIE: It's just that I couldn't pass this up. I was waiting in line for hours at the Bangor Best Buy Book Sellers, that's where I get all your first editions. The woman there was not helpful at all…

KING: So I've been told.

QUEENIE: But I met this nice young man who was picking up a copy for you. So I—

KING: You followed him.

QUEENIE: Yes. I followed him. Lucky I had my car with me by golly that boy can run!

KING: Gimme your book.

QUEENIE: Oh, yes, yes here!

She hands him her book and he signs it

KING: Who do I make it out to?

QUEENIE: Your number one fan.

KING: Is there a name that goes with that?

QUEENIE: (dismissive) Annie. Annie Wilkes. But I'm a plain jane nobody, not the Hollywood type you're so used to gallivant-ing 'round with; I mean all those glamorous pretty ladies and the parties and the big important producers and the like; I'm just some silly goat stuck out on her big ole farm down the road; you don't need to pollute your masterpiece with my name…

KING: (writing) To Annie Wilkes. My number one fan. Lots of love Stephen King.

Queenie is astounded. She is completely star struck. She collects her book as if it were the lost scrolls of the holy bible

QUEENIE: Thank you. Oh my goodness, heavens to Betsy, thank you so much…

KING: You're welcome Annie.

King sits back at his typewriter, Queenie hovers over him, worshipping him but also slowly morphing into something monstrous:

QUEENIE: This is just too much for me. Really it is. I've loved you from day one. From the short stories you wrote for Playboy magazine to your articles and your essays and all those anthologies…

KING: Thank you, you're too kind.

QUEENIE: Oh but the novels! My my those are just too good for words!

KING: Oh no, they're word worthy alright.

QUEENIE: I'm just in awe of your genius. You are a god among men.

KING: I might have to hire you. Keep you around the place. Sayin' exactly the stuff it is you're saying.

QUEENIE: So what's the new book about?

KING: Haven't really decided yet.

QUEENIE: Oh I'd love to sit here and watch you write.

KING: That might make me a tad nervous.

QUEENIE: Oh I won't be a bother, I just want to be in control of, I mean, I just want to be involved or see how your mind works…sorry I'm hopeless. The right words never come out for me and I just seem all over the shop and—

KING: Do you want a drink?

QUEENIE: Oh no no no not me! I don't drink!

KING: Well do you mind if I do?

QUEENIE: Not at all. Why would I?

KING: I think I'm gonna like you.

QUEENIE: Oh! You're so lovely! I read that you were a charming and decent fellah in many a magazine but they can write whatever it is they want really, you have to actually meet the celebrity up close and personal to really know that they're nice. And you haven't disappointed at all... you really are nice.

KING: You got me on a good day.

QUEENIE: (in love) Oh I just love your writing Paul, it's just so—noble.

KING: (puzzled) Paul?

Princess enters the scene; Queenie remains there but hidden in darkness staring at King waiting for him to pound the typewriter

Princess is her ditsy dog-walking self again. But this time she seems a tad solemn:

KING: Hey. How was the walk?

PRINCESS: Good.

KING: They have fun?

PRINCESS: They always do.

KING: Hey you're not ranting, something the matter?

PRINCESS: Do I rant?

KING: You usually trail off without stopping to breathe and right now you ain't. You not yourself today.

PRINCESS: No. I'm not.

KING: What's up?

PRINCESS: Oh nothing.

KING: Come on let me in.

PRINCESS: The dogs and me went to Max's Café.

KING: Where they let dogs in the beer garden, right?

PRINCESS: Yeah.

KING: And?

PRINCESS: And the TV was on.

KING: So?

PRINCESS: Mr King there was an accident.

KING: I think I just had one of those too...

He begins to scratch out something he wrote

PRINCESS: In Portland. A car accident.

KING: Portland? Is anyone hurt?

PRINCESS: It was just on the news. I had to tell you as soon as I heard. I got scared Mr King. For the first time in my life I really got scared.

KING: So you've been lying to me all this time? You never got remotely white knuckled readin' one of my fucking books? Jeesh!

PRINCESS: When I heard about the accident in Portland my mind went wandering and I got thinking. I had an image flash in my head and a thought that hung there like a bad smell. A horrible thought.

KING: Bring it on dear, maybe I can rip it off…

PRINCESS: Imagine if that was Tabitha.

King is distracted from his work now:

KING: Oh Christ.

PRINCESS: No, really, imagine if it was.

KING: Hey! It wasn't so stop saying it.

PRINCESS: Oh fuck Mr. King what would you do if that happened? Where would you end up? How would you cope?

KING: Leave it alone. Tabby is fine. She's perfectly ok.

PRINCESS: And imagine if it was one of your kids.

KING: Enough. I don't want to imagine…

PRINCESS: Imagine instead of that little nameless girl from Connecticut lying there on that asphalt bleeding internally and sporting large gaping wounds with her lifeless body ready for decomposition and her face bruised to a pulp it was one of your own. It was Joe! Your little boy!

KING: I don't want to think about that. My kids are gonna live forever.

PRINCESS: Just picture it. What would you do? How would you cope? How *could* you cope?

KING: (stumped) Ahh—I-I couldn't.

QUEENIE: But you'd have to. Wouldn't you?

KING: Get out of my house.

QUEENIE: I don't think so Paul.

Queenie gets up. She is frightening. She retrieves a large mallet from near by. It was hiding all this time. She thumps into her open palm staring at King

KING: I'm not Paul, who the fuck is Paul?

QUEENIE: I don't like how you've been writing.

KING: You don't have a say.

QUEENIE: I don't?

KING: No!

QUEENIE: I'm your biggest fan Paul. I need to have the final say.

KING: Stop calling me Paul!

QUEENIE: But you are Paul Sheldon. The world famous romance novelist. My favorite novelist. My darling Paul Sheldon...

KING: I'm not no fucking romance novelist you crazy bitch!

QUEENIE: Now Paul is that the way to speak to your number one fan? Especially when I saved you from that freak accident? You could have been stuck in that snow. The police wouldn't of found you for days!

KING: What the fuck is going on?

QUEENIE: Write what *I* see is fit Paul, that's how things are gonna work from here on in.

KING: (typing) So the writer, angry and agitated and frustrated and fucking pissed off grabs hold of the mother fucking axe and in one swift mother fucking move he slices the goddamn mother fucking head off his biggest fucking fan!

Queenie brings the mallet down straight onto King's legs and he screams in agony

She does this again; his scream is even more intense

QUEENIE: There's no nobility in that kind of talk Paul.

KING: (screaming in pain) Jeeeeeeesus!

QUEENIE: And stop using the Lord's name in vein. (to Jesus) Forgive him Father for he knows not what he does.

Mr Knight and Princeton appear. Mr Knight is stern faced and sad. He is telling Princeton some bad news:

MR KNIGHT: This is the worst part of my job Mr King. I don't know how to say this...

KING: That's not me.

QUEENIE: (cold) Yes it is.

PRINCESS: (sobbing) It is...it is...

PRINCETON: What is it, just tell me for God's sake?

MR KNIGHT: The snow was heavy on the freeway and your wife's car was just—

KING: That's not me!

MR KNIGHT: Mr. King, your wife and children were found days later...

PRINCETON: Stop it!

KING: Yeah stop it!

PRINCETON: What are you saying?

MR. KNIGHT: your wife and children are dead Mr. King. I'm dreadfully sorry.

PRINCETON: Oh God!

KING: Stop it that's not me!

PRINCESS: I wish it wasn't but it is, it is...

KING: Enough! For fuck's sake this has to end now!

PRINCESS: How will you cope? How *could* you cope?

QUEENIE: Write them out of the story Paul.

KING: Get the fuck out of here…

QUEENIE: You need to write them out. It will benefit the book.

PRINCETON: (grim) I know a place. It's beyond the path. I can bury Tabby and the kids there and they'll come back, I just know it. It worked with my cat. He's fine and dandy now…

PRINCESS: Take them there. Dig them out of their graves and take them there.

PRINCETON: It's an ancient Indian burial ground I know about.

MR KNIGHT: Sometimes dead is better Mr. King.

QUEENIE: Exactly. Kill them off. Don't you dare start typing their names. They don't need to be mentioned ever again. You just type these six final words: His wife and kids were dead! You kill them off then you can be mine for good.

MR KNIGHT: It's all about mixing up your play time with your wok time Jack.

PRINCETON: I buried them in the Pet Sematary.

PRINCESS: Good work. They'll come back. They always come back.

KING: Good work.

QUEENIE: No! You don't bring them back from the dead you hack! You let them go! Let them die!

KING: No! I can't! I won't!

QUEENIE: Bury them and forget 'em, let 'em rot in the earth, that's what needs to happen…that's what you're supposed to write!

KING: I'm not writing that!

QUEENIE: Yes you are.

KING: No!

QUEENIE: If you don't there'll be hell to pay! Your biggest fan demands you kill them off!

She slams his legs again

KING: (in agony) I don't give a flying fuck what my biggest fan wants!

QUEENIE: You should and you will! Now write it! Write!

PRINCETON: Come home Tabby, come home kids! Come back home to daddy!

MR KNIGHT: All work and no play…

PRINCESS: Save them Mr. King…

QUEENIE: Write them out of the story, it will benefit the book, now write, write, write, write!

The frenzy dies down. Stephen King relaxes

The others fade out into darkness. We can still hear their voices:

PRINCESS: A telekinetic teen.

PRINCETON: A demonic car.

MR KNIGHT: A haunted hotel.

QUEENIE: A pet cemetery.

The phone rings

King picks it up

KING: Hello? (beat then relief) Ahh Tabby honey how are you? (beat) To get to Portland ok? Good to hear. How'm I doin? Why does everyone ask that? Ha ha. Yeah baby I'm doin' fine. How are the kids? Good. I'm glad. Hope they don't have too much fun up there…Portland's more deathly dull than this place for the lil' bastards. Work? Oh yeah, its comin' along real nicely. (a long beat) Yeah sweetheart.

KING: Thanks for calling and letting me know you're all safe and what not. I'll speak to you soon. Love ya. Bye.

He hangs up and goes to his desk

He picks up a bottle and begins to pour. But stops half way and then collects everything and puts it away

He then sits back down; back at his god, and begins to type. Slowly at first, then the rhythms pick up speed and a work is in progress

The end

Curtain call all in unison; all together

About Lee Gambin

A Melbourne, Australia based playwright, screenwriter, film and theatre essayist and journalist for famed USA horror film magazine Fangoria Lee Gambin has worked in independent theatre for many years as well as Artistic Director of his own independent theatre company. He has worked as a lecturer for numerous film societies and film festivals including the Melbourne International Film Festival, the Analyzing Genre Program, Movie Maniacs Intl. and is in current collaboration with famous institutions such as American International Pictures and Famous Monsters of Filmland.

Special Note Regarding Production of the Play

King of Bangor is a one act play written by Lee Gambin and is readily available for production by theatre companies (both established and independent) or theatrically involved individuals.

As a five-hander with minimal sets and costumes, the play is an extremely appropriate and manageable one for many theatre companies and individuals. We most definitely encourage performers and production companies to take on this highly dramatic piece.

Please send your request to perform the play to Mr Gambin at gambinsgoregalore666@gmail.com

Royalties can be worked out with the author via email.

Thank you

MONSTROUS

2010 VOL. 1 NO. 1

THE OVERLOOK CONNECTION
BOOKSTORE OF THE FANTASTIC

STEPHEN KING

CATALOG

IN THIS ISSUE

FRANK DARABONT

THE MIST CAST

ON THE MIST SET

The MIST Special Issue!!!

INSIDE: Everything Stephen King !
Books ! Video ! Audio ! Ephemera !

StephenKingCatalog.com !

www.ingramcontent.com/pod-product-compliance
Lightning Source LLC
Chambersburg PA
CBHW031527040426
42445CB00009B/433